W9-AMB-353

CHRISTMAS MEMORIES

Publications International, Ltd.

Cover and interior art: Library of Congress, Shutterstock.com

Copyright © 2016 Publications International, Ltd. All rights reserved.
This book may not be reproduced or quoted in whole or in part by any
means whatsoever without written permission from:

Louis Weber, CEO
Publications International, Ltd.
8140 Lehigh Avenue
Morton Grove, IL 60053

Permission is never granted for commercial purposes.

ISBN: 978-1-68022-642-3

Manufactured in China.

8 7 6 5 4 3 2 1

Introduction

The Christmas season is full of family, food, gifts, and laughter. And, of course, it's full of memories, from childhood toys to longstanding family and cultural traditions. *Christmas Memories* celebrates the season with Christmas jokes and anecdotes to make you laugh, quotations to make you think, and stories to warm your heart. You'll be reminded of toys that were that year's Christmas craze and find out about holiday traditions in the past and around the world. These memories might even spark your own, so you can share these stories and your own memories with your family and friends, and find out anew how wonderful the Christmas season is! ★

Christmas Quotes

The best Christmas of all is the presence of a happy family all wrapped up with one another.

—Author Unknown ❄

Christmas! 'Tis the season for kindling the fire of hospitality in the hall, the genial fire of charity in the heart.

—Washington Irving ❄

Where It All Started

The origins of many Christmas traditions are a bit vague, but we can actually date the first commercial Christmas card. It was printed in England in 1843, using illustrations by John Calcott Horsley, a noted London artist of the time. He was commissioned by Henry Cole, a busy businessman who worked in the Public Records Office in London. He was so busy, in fact, that he didn't have time to write individual letters to all of his friends, family, and business acquaintances at Christmastime. The press run was 1,000 cards. Today, in the United States alone, two billion cards are sent every Christmas—which is something of a hallmark. ✳

To

A MERRY CHRISTMAS
AND
A HAPPY NEW YEAR
TO YOU

Published at Summerly's Home Treasury Office.   From

On the front of the card, Horsley created a triptych. The side panels depicted acts of charity: feeding the hungry and clothing the naked. The center panel showed a happy family embracing, drinking wine, and frolicking in a merry party.

I'm Dreaming of a White (House) Christmas... 1923

The first National Christmas Tree was a 48-foot balsam fir, erected by the District of Columbia Public Schools on the Ellipse south of the White House in November 1923. About 3,000 spectators gathered that Christmas Eve at 5:00 P.M. to watch President Calvin Coolidge and his wife, Grace, stroll from the White House to the tree. The president then pressed a button to activate the 2,500 electric red, green, and white bulbs on the tree, winning cheers and applause from the cold but excited crowd. Coolidge was especially pleased that the tree came from his home state of Vermont. 🌲

Coolidge lights the community Christmas tree in 1923.

Christmas became an official U.S. holiday when it was signed into law in 1870 by President Ulysses S. Grant. It wasn't until 1890 that every state followed suit and declared it a holiday.

Coolidge was the first president to preside over a community Christmas tree, but in 1856, Franklin Pierce became the first president to place a Christmas tree in the White House. ✳

. . . .

Christmas is not a time nor a season, but a state of mind. To cherish peace and goodwill, to be plenteous in mercy, is to have the real spirit of Christmas.

—Calvin Coolidge ❄

First Lady Grace Coolidge with a Christmas basket

Bulletin Blunders

Christmas: a time when churches are crowded, and the church newsletter may contain some unintended entertainment, as these excerpts show…

* After eating Christmas dinner, join us in the church hall for a Christmas concert. The choir will open with "O Come All Ye Facefull."

* The director of the Christmas pageant is still looking for wise men. No experience necessary.

* Will all of those with rolls in the church Christmas play please report to the kitchen after the service.

Crunching the Christmas Numbers

200: Number of mincemeat pies eaten by Gus the camel after breaking out of his pen at an Irish school's Christmas party. He also drank several cans of Guinness, which he opened with his teeth.

28: Average number of Christmas cards each U.S. household mails each year

1948: Year the Marine Corps adopted the Toys for Tots program

2 million: Number of visitors expected at *Christkindlesmarkt,* the famous Christmas market in Nuremberg, Germany

3: Number of gifts the magi presented to the baby Jesus, according to the Bible

1,300: Costumes worn during the Radio City Music Hall Christmas Spectacular

Babe Ruth, Santa Claus?

There is a famous photograph that shows Babe Ruth surrounded by what seems like a hundred clamoring children, yet that moon face and huge grin under the straw boater are unmistakable for their goofy brightness. Ruth was in his element, surrounded by his biggest fans and most star struck admirers, and he was loving every minute of it.

Throughout his career, after ball games and at special appearances, Ruth spent up to several hours at a time signing autographs. He couldn't bear the thought of any tyke going home disappointed. In New York and on the road as well, the Babe frequently visited hospitals to help cheer up sick children. In 1931 alone, he played Santa Claus for

hundreds of kids at city hospitals. He also spent a lot of time visiting orphanages—probably because he basically grew up at Saint Mary's Industrial School for Boys, an orphanage in Baltimore.

By 1947, when Ruth could no longer deliver joy to fans with his majestic home runs and, in fact, could barely walk, one thing he still could do was make children happy. That December, the cancer-stricken Ruth painfully pulled on a Santa Claus suit, beard and all, and handed out presents to young victims of polio at the Hotel Astor in New York. As their faces lit up, it was clear their delight gave Babe much joy. Afterward, he pulled down his beard and addressed the cameras and microphones. Though his voice was subdued and raspy, he spoke with the utmost sincerity. "I want to take this opportunity," he said, "to wish all the children—not only in America, but all over the world—a very merry Christmas." 🎄

Christmas Quotes

*I heard the bells on Christmas day
Their old familiar carols play,
And wild and sweet the words repeat
Of peace on earth, good will to men.
Then pealed the bells more loud and deep:
God is not dead, nor doth he sleep;
The wrong shall fail, the right prevail,
With peace on earth, good will to men.*

—Henry Wadsworth Longfellow ✻

*Selfishness makes Christmas a burden;
love makes it a delight.*

—Anonymous ✻

Under the Christmas Tree: 1945

he idea for the Slinky was born when naval engineer Richard James knocked over a spring he was working with and watched it "slink" down from shelf to table to floor before recoiling to a stop. He started a company to make the toys and convinced Gimbels department store in Philadelphia to let him demonstrate them during the 1945 Christmas season. Within 90 minutes of setting up his display, all 400 Slinkies he had made were sold for a dollar each. 🎄

Christmas Babies

Ask any kid with a Christmas birthday and they'll inform you that no matter how much their parents try to make up for it, it just stinks. Even if they get twice as many presents, two days of celebration are reduced to one, and there's really no getting around it. These famous Christmas babies could tell you all about it:

✳ Humphrey Bogart (1899), actor

✳ Sissy Spacek (1949), actor

✳ Rod Serling (1924), playwright and producer. One of the most memorable episodes of his brilliant and beloved science-fiction television show, *The Twilight Zone,* is "Night of the Meek," in which Art Carney gives a tour-de-force performance as Henry Corwin,

a drunken Santa who is suddenly given the power to help the poor and downtrodden.

✳ Annie Lennox (1954), singer. If Lennox ever felt bitterness about her Christmas birthday, she must have gotten over it by the time she recorded Eurythmics' popular version of "Winter Wonderland" in 1987 for the Special Olympics benefit album *A Very Special Christmas.*

✳ Jimmy Buffett (1946), singer. He released an album called *Christmas Island* in 1996. Though there are a few traditional tunes on it, such as "Jingle Bells" and "I'll Be Home for Christmas," Buffett puts his own tropical stamp on the album with "A Sailor's Christmas," "Mele Kalikimaka," and "Ho Ho Ho and a Bottle of Rhum."

The Legend of the Poinsettia

The people of Mexico have long credited Pepita, a poor Mexican girl, with the origin of the poinsettia. When she was to approach the Christ child and present a gift one Christmas Eve, she was wrought with sadness by the fact that she had no gift to offer. "Even the most humble gift, if given in love, will be acceptable in his eyes," consoled her cousin, Pedro.

Pepita considered his advice, then gathered a handful of common weeds. Still, she grew embarrassed by her scraggly offering and cried, but she remembered her cousin's thoughtful words as she knelt at the manger in the nativity scene. Suddenly, the bouquet of weeds bloomed a brilliant red, and it was proclaimed by all who saw it to be a Christmas

miracle. Since that fabled Christmas Eve night, the red flowers have been known as ***Flores de Noche Buena,*** or Flowers of the Holy Night, since they bloom yearly during the Christmas season.

In 1828, Joel Roberts Poinsett, the first United States Ambassador to Mexico and a novice botanist, scoured the Mexican countryside in his free time in search of interesting, new plant species. He found a brilliant shrub with large red flowers growing wild next to a roadside. With cuttings he brought back to his greenhouse in South Carolina, Poinsett cultivated plants to give as gifts. In doing so, his famed reputation as a statesman was eventually overshadowed by his Christmas gift to all future generations: the poinsettia.

Poinsettia Facts

✳ Over 70 million poinsettia plants are sold throughout the United States each year, making the poinsettia the number one flowering potted plant sold.

✳ Poinsettias are NOT poisonous but they do have an acrid, bitter taste. The plant is not harmful to pets, either, though it can cause a tummy ache.

✳ Poinsettias are warm weather tropical plants. In their native Central America and Mexico, they grow as shrubs and can reach up to 10 feet tall. Though they are best known as Christmas plants, they can-not withstand cold temperatures but thrive best inside at room temperature.

✳ The most popular color for poinsettias is the traditional red, but they are also available in white, cream, pink, and yellow and can be striped, spotted, or marbled (or even spraypainted other colors).

✳ Poinsettias don't have flowers. Instead, their leaves, called bracts, give the plant its colorful appearance. About eight weeks before Christmas, nurseries place the plants in complete darkness for at least 14 hours a day to force the bracts to change color. Because the ratio of sunlight hours to darkness triggers the coloration, the longer the plants are left in darkness, the brighter their leaves.

Christmas Tree Traditions

The contemporary Christmas tree originated in 16th-century Germany, when devout Christians put up triangular trees (possibly to represent the holy trinity). Observing how beautiful the stars looked twinkling through the branches of an evergreen tree, Protestant reformer Martin Luther came up with lighting the tree using candles to create a similar effect. That remained the tradition until the late 19th century, when Thomas Edison developed miniature electric lights to string on trees.

The tree custom arrived in America in the 18th century with the German immigrants. Americans viewed the tree with skepticism as a pagan symbol, until a British paper showed royal "It" girl,

Christmas tree market, taken late 1800s

Queen Victoria, posing around a decorated Christmas tree in 1846. Suddenly, the English as well as fashionable East Coast Americans simply had to have a Christmas tree.

The first Christmas tree lot opened in Manhattan in 1851. Today 30 million Christmas trees are sold in the United States every year—fake trees not included. 🎄

How the Christmas tree got to England

You might be surprised to learn how relatively new the Christmas tree is to jolly olde England and how it arrived on British shores as a result of one of that country's most legendary romances.

Queen Victoria ascended to the throne of England on June 20, 1837, at the tender age of 18. Her uncle, King William IV, had died of heart failure, leaving behind only the ten illegitimate children he had sired with the actress Dorothea Jordan. Victoria was a confident young woman, and though she could hardly be called a feminist, she had no doubt in her leadership abilities as a woman. Still, like generations of women after her, she longed to "have it all." Taking a husband and bearing children was a monarch's

duty, of course, but it was a duty she was happy to fulfill. She would have married out of political obligation alone if it had come to that, but instead she was lucky enough to find happiness in that rarest of relationships: a royal love match.

Unions between first cousins were nothing out of the ordinary in those days, especially among royals and aristocrats, so Victoria felt no need to hold back her feelings upon meeting her cousin Prince Albert of Saxe-Coburg and Gotha. The young German prince was handsome, kind, and intelligent, and Victoria quickly fell in love. She also knew that the sooner she married, the sooner she would be out from under the control of her domineering mother, with whom, as a proper 19th-century young lady, she was required to live. They were married on February 10, 1840. Albert's new, formal title was His Royal Highness Prince Albert.

An 1848 engraving titled "Christmas tree at Windsor Castle"

Like Victoria, Albert was eager to start his own family, perhaps because his childhood had been full of heartache. His parents, Ernest I, Duke of Saxe-Coburg-Saalfeld, and Louise of Saxe-Gotha-Altenburg, had fought constantly over their infidelities. Many historians believe that Albert was the biological son of Baron von Mayern, the chamberlain at the court of Saxe-Coburg-Gotha. When Albert was seven years old, his parents mercifully divorced, and he settled into a comfortable life of study and play. But he was never allowed to see his mother again, surely a terrible ordeal for any small child to go through. Albert clung to the things he still had, and two of those things were German culture and the Lutheran Evangelical Church.

The newlyweds Victoria and Albert were blissfully happy and very much in love, but Albert was homesick. Though still a Protestant, he'd obviously been forced to leave Lutheranism for the Church

of England when he'd married the Defender of the Faith. And so many other things were different, too, including the language, eating and drinking habits, and child-rearing methods. Albert felt out of his element, and Victoria noticed that this homesickness hit him especially hard during religious holidays. She encouraged him to keep his German traditions, even if he had to practice them far from home.

Though the Christmas tree was not unheard of in England (the gossipy diarist Henry Greville recounted that the German Princess Lieven decorated three at her 1827 holiday party in London) the English had shown no interest in adopting this German symbol for themselves. That all changed 13 years later when Victoria and Albert began their family, and Albert placed a Christmas tree, with presents beneath it, in the nursery for their children.

The British press eagerly reported this cozy scene, the English promptly fell in love with the Christmas tree, and what was at first thought a "fad" is now a beloved institution. ✳

Which Carol?

Check out these lines, and see if you can pick out which popular carols and songs they come from.

1. We won't go until we get some, so bring it right here
a. "Blue Christmas"
b. "Here We Come A-Wassailing"
c. "We Wish You a Merry Christmas"
d. "I Only Want You for Christmas"

2. We'll take a cup of kindness yet
a. "Here We Come A-Wassailing"
b. "Auld Lang Syne"
c. "Mistletoe and Wine"
d. "God Rest Ye Merry Gentlemen"

3. Please, Please, Please, Please
a. "Please Come Home for Christmas"

b. "Nuttin' for Christmas"
c. "Santa Baby"
d. "Baby Please Come Home"

4. I'm filling my stocking with a duplex
a. "Deck the Halls"
b. "Santa Baby"
c. "Let It Snow"
d. "The Magic of Christmas Day"

5. Snowing and blowing up bushels of fun
a. "Frosty the Snowman"
b. "White Christmas"
c. "Boogie Woogie Santa Claus"
d. "Jingle Bell Rock"

6. Is the pudding done?
a. "Baby Please Come Home"
b. "Over the River"
c. "It Feels Like Christmas"
d. "Sugar Plum Fairies"

The Gold Wrapping Paper

The popular Christmas story tells the tale of a father who came home to find that his young daughter had used all the expensive gold wrapping paper, meant for gifts to the extended family, to decorate a large shoebox that she'd put under the Christmas tree. He was a little upset about this—money was tight that Christmas—but swallowed it down.

On Christmas morning, his little girl brought the gift over to him and said, "This is for you!" The father expected some small treasure. Instead, the box was completely empty. In an outburst of anger, the father said harshly, "I don't believe you used the good

wrapping paper for something that isn't even a gift. Gifts shouldn't be empty!"

His daughter, crushed, looked up at him and said, "But it's not empty. I blew kisses into it until it was completely full!"

The father deeply regretted his anger. He apologized and hugged his daughter, knowing that the best gift he could have was her love.

A short time later, the child passed away in a car accident. For the rest of his life, the father would look inside his gold-wrapped shoebox when he needed to remember his daughter's smile and her abundant and generous love. 🎄

Curious Classifieds

You see the strangest things advertised around Christmas…

* Semi-Annual after-Christmas Sale

* Christmas tag sale. Handmade gifts for the hard-to-find person.

* Artificial Christmas Tree For Sale. Like New. Needs stand, ornaments, lights and branches. $99.00 firm.

Crunching the
Christmas Numbers

2,314: Number of people who live in Santa Claus, Indiana

1223: Year that St. Francis of Assisi first displayed a crèche, or miniature nativity scene, in Grecchio, Italy

1892: Year *The Nutcracker* was first performed at the Mariinsky Theatre of Russia

100 million: Number of copies of the song "White Christmas" that have sold around the world

594 million: Value in dollars of imported Christmas tree ornaments from China

1931: Year the Christmas tree first appeared on the site of Rockefeller Center in New York

Cola Claus?

Nothing says "Christmas" like the image of a white-whiskered fat man in a red suit squeezing down a chimney with a sack full of toys. But Santa Claus hasn't always looked that way. When the Coca-Cola Company used the red-robed figure in the 1930s to promote its soft drinks, the classic image of Santa was cemented in the public consciousness.

Santa Claus evolved from two religious figures, St. Nicholas and Christkindlein. St. Nicholas was a real person, a monk who became a bishop in the early fourth century and was renowned as a generous gift-giver. Christkindlein (meaning "Christ child") was assisted by elfin helpers and would leave gifts for children while they slept.

Santa plays the tunes in this 1889 illustration from Nast

The chimney in the illustration bears a sign that reads "Santa Claus stop here."

Santa Claus originated from a Dutch poem, "Sinterklaas," and the legend was added to over time by different writers. Until the early 20th century, though, Santa Claus was portrayed in many different ways. He could be tall and clad in long robes like St. Nicholas, or small with whiskers like the elves who helped Christkindlein.

In 1881, Thomas Nast, a caricaturist for *Harper's Weekly*, first drew Santa as a merry figure in red with flowing whiskers, an image close to the one we know today. Printer Louis Prang used a similar image in 1885 when he introduced Christmas cards to America. In 1931, the Coca-Cola Company first employed Haddon Sundblom to illustrate its annual advertisements, choosing a Santa dressed in red and white to match the corporate colors. By then, however, this was already the most popular image of Santa Claus, one that was described in detail in a *New York Times* article in 1927. If Coca-Cola had really

invented Santa Claus, children would likely be saving the milk and leaving him soda and cookies on Christmas Eve.

· ·

Speaking of holiday icons, Rudolph the Red-nosed Reindeer was born 100 years later than the rest of his reindeer pals. This shiny-nosed hero of Christmas was created in 1939 by Robert L. May, a copywriter for Montgomery Ward, as an advertising gimmick. ✳

CAUGHT!

This Nast image from c. 1892 is titled "Caught!"

Pere Fouettard

We Americans have been known to make fun of the French, but when it comes to Christmas and kids, they're actually a lot more hardcore than we are. Sure, we say our Santa keeps an eye on who's naughty and nice, but it's obvious we've had enforcement issues for centuries. The naughty American kids aren't worried about not getting presents. They aren't losing any sleep about finding coal in their stockings on Christmas morning. Well, not so in France, my friend. Those French kids are shaking in their footie pajamas.

You know those action movies that feature a "good cop" and a "bad cop"? That's how it goes down in France during the Christmas season. Pere Noel, Father Christmas, is the good cop. And the bad cop?

Oh, that would be a fellow named Pere Fouettard, who dresses in black and carries a whip.

Not only is he tough, but he'll snitch when he has to. Heck, snitching is his job. He keeps a list of all the naughty *enfants* in France and then runs and tattles to Pere Noel. Pere Noel is the boss, the captain, and he don't want to get his hands dirty, see? But with Pere Fouettard around, his rep stays as clean as whistle, and all the kids keep giving him *beaucoup d'amour*. C'est bien, eh? ♠

Hoover lighting the community Christmas tree in 1930—no fires that year!

I'm Dreaming of a White (House) Christmas... 1929

An ill-timed flu bug, an overcooked turkey—we've all had Christmases that were less than ideal. Even the president isn't immune. On Christmas Eve 1929, the White House caught fire while President Hoover was hosting a children's party. The culprit was a chimney flue. (Given that the building has more than two dozen wood-burning fireplaces, it's a wonder more fires haven't started over the years.) The fire gutted the Oval Office and the West Wing. ✳

Under the Christmas Tree: 1975

Maybe it could only have happened in the 1970s. California advertising executive Gary Dahl decided that a rock would make a perfect no-fuss, no-mess, no-walk pet. He packaged polished stones on piles of straw inside boxes with holes, wrote a book called the "Pet Rock Training Manual" and started selling them in August 1975 at a gift show in San Francisco for $3.95. Dahl announced his toy with a press release sent to major media outlets. *Newsweek* magazine carried an article about it, newspapers ran stories, and Johnny Carson featured it on *The Tonight Show*. The fad ended after Christmas 1975, but the phrase "pet rock" lives on. 🌲

Christmas Laughs

On Christmas day, Mom and Dad thought it would be a great idea to have their small son say grace. They were proud when their son started off by saying thanks for their family, his baby sister, and Grandpa and Grandma. He even remembered to thank God for the food! Roast beef, mashed potatoes, jello, the Christmas cookies and pie planned for dessert…then there was a long pause.

"Are you all done, honey?" his mom asked. "Should we say Amen?"

The little boy looked seriously at her and said, "Do I have to thank God for the broccoli? I think he'll know I'm lying!" ✷

Christmas with Henry VIII

S o what was in a Christmas dinner fit for a king? Here are some of the items served at feasts during that time…

✳ **Boar's Head:** A boar's head, garnished with bay and rosemary, served as the centerpiece of Christmas feasts. It certainly outdoes a floral display.

✳ **Whole Roasted Peacock:** This delicacy was served dressed in its own iridescent blue feathers (which were plucked, then replaced after the bird had been cooked), with its beak gilded in gold leaf. Roasted swan was another treat reserved for special occasions, as swans were regarded as too noble and dignified for everyday consumption.

✳ Spiced Fruitcake: Desserts weren't very popular in England until the 18th century, when elaborate sugar sculptures became popular among the aristocracy.

The exception to the no dessert rule was during the Twelfth Night banquet on January 6 (the end of the Christmas season), when a special spiced fruitcake containing a dried pea or bean was served. Whoever found the pea would be king or queen of the pea or bean and was treated as a guest of honor for the remainder of the evening. ♣

A Rocky Christmas

Santa had to compete for airspace on Christmas Eve 1965, when Britain's largest meteorite sent thousands of fragments showering down on Barwell, Leicestershire. Museums immediately started offering money for fragments of the rock, causing the previously sleepy town to be inundated with meteorite hunters and other adventurers from around the world. Decades later, the phenomenon continues to captivate meteorite enthusiasts, and fragments can often be found for sale online. ✳

Antebellum Greased Lightning: The Story Behind Jingle Bells

When James Pierpont copyrighted "One Horse Open Sleigh" in 1857, there is no way he could have known that he had written one of the most popular Christmas songs of all time.

Pierpont rechristened his song "Jingle Bells" two years later, but the only part of the song he changed was the title, leaving us with lyrics that, today, are often misunderstood or forgotten altogether. In fact, the song has more to do with horse-drawn street racing and picking up antebellum babes than any holiday. The first two verses almost everyone knows.

Dashing thro' the snow,
In a one horse open sleigh,
O'er the hills we go,
Laughing all the way;
Bells on bob tail ring,
Making spirits bright,
Oh what sport to ride and sing
A sleighing song tonight.
A day or two ago
I tho't I'd take a ride
And soon Miss Fannie Bright
Was seated by my side,
The horse was lean and lank
Misfortune seem'd his lot
He got into a drifted bank
And we—we got up sot.

• •

Most of us don't think much about those lyrics, but
no one can deny that there isn't a single mention of

Christmas. Pierpont describes his date with a young woman, wherein he speeds around in an open-top sleigh driven by a sleek horse with a stylishly bobbed tail. Further, the horse is decked out with jingling bells, so we know he has the pre-Civil War equivalent of a "hot ride." The holiday season isn't mentioned once. Even though he totals his pony-roadster in a snowdrift, he and his girl still have a great time. Horse-powered roadster? If the first two verses make you think of Sandy and Zuko going out for a night on the town, then surely the last two are Kenickie's ode to greaser life in the 19th century. Pierpont's oft-ignored next lyrics go:

A day or two ago,
The story I must tell
I went out on the snow
And on my back I fell;
A gent was riding by
In a one horse open sleigh,

He laughed as there I sprawling lie,
But quickly drove away.
Now the ground is white,
Go it while you're young,
Take the girls to night
And sing this sleighing song;
Just get a bob-tailed bay
Two forty as his speed
Hitch him to an open sleigh
And crack, you'll take the lead.

· ·

When he falls on his bum in the snow, a fellow road-ster can't help but laugh and speed off. Then, as if to change the subject, he tells us that we should go out, pick up some girls, and try it ourselves. He spells out just how fast the horse should be, and what color and tail-style we should get! Translating for those who are nonequestrian-inclined, a "bob-tailed bay" is a reddish-brown horse whose tail has been

cut short. This is Pierpont's version of purple taillights and 30-inch fins. Also, "two forty" refers to a mile in 2 minutes and 40 seconds. Burning up the quarter-mile might not have anything to do with Christmas, but "Jingle Bells" is still about enjoying the winter season and is one of the most loved holiday songs of all time. 🌲

Don't Neigh-Say This Idea!

Do you buy Christmas presents for your animal companions? You're not alone in that! And if you had a horse in the 1910s and 1920s, you could have brought them to a special Christmas tree during the holiday season. A contemporary picture caption described the occasion as, "The annual Christmas tree for horses provided by the Animal rescue league in Washington, D.C. In addition to the Christmas tree which was hung with apples, ears of corn and other horse dainties, well filled nose bags were provided." Maybe next year you can have a "doggie" Christmas tree that supplies your pooch with kibble, squeaky toys, and bones? ✳

Christmas Laughs

D on went to the department store to buy his wife a gift for Christmas. He ended up at the perfume counter. "How about a nice perfume?" he asked the clerk.

She pulled out a bottle, saying, "This is a big seller, very popular, very classy."

"Hmm," Don said, seeing the price tag for $60. "What are some other options? Some less expensive options."

She showed him one for $30.

"That's still a lot of money for a pretty small bottle," Don replied. "What do you have for less than that?"

Christmas shoppers at Woolworth's five and ten cent store, 1941

With a frown, the clerk pulled out an even smaller bottle. "This is only $10," she said.

"Well…what about you show me something real cheap?"

The clerk sighed, reached down under the counter, and handed him a mirror. 🎄

Under the Christmas Tree: 1966

The hottest game of Christmas 1966, in more ways than one, was Twister. The first game to use humans as board pieces, Twister players tie themselves in knots by putting their hands and feet on colored dots until someone can't reach or the players fall over. Invented by Charles F. Foley and Neil Rabens, Twister was produced by Milton Bradley and was unofficially introduced to the United States in May 1966 when Johnny Carson and actress Eva Gabor, wearing a low-cut dress, demonstrated it on *The Tonight Show*. Over three million Twister games were sold in its first year. ✳

Out of the Mouths of Babes...

✸ Little Wayne could always be found sitting under the Christmas tree singing his favorite song: "A Wayne in the Manger."

✸ Ray carefully folded a paper airplane and put it next to the figure on the top of the Christmas tree. "He's a Blue Angel," he explained.

A Christmas Memory

My great aunt was a joyful person. She understood kids, and when our family visited each Christmas, she always had a craft planned. We created Christmas ornaments from felt and milkweed pods. We baked bread. It was only when I grew older that I understood the challenges she faced over the years, including the loss of a son to a car accident. And yet she patiently built a happy life around the grief, and knew how to share joy. For my great aunt, happiness was a life skill. She truly put the idea of "joy to the world" into action. 🌲

Christmas Movie Anagrams

Rearrange the letters of the phrases below to find famous Christmas movie titles.

1. FAST RUINED LOWLIFE

2. SHH, WARTIME TICS

3. RED NOSE HELPED HERD TO RIDE, RUN

4. 'TIS AS CHARCOAL, MR.

People packing Christmas gifts to be send to children in Europe affected by World War I, 1914

Christmas Peace

On Christmas Day in 1914, an impromptu truce interrupted World War I, and combatants from both sides briefly met as friends in No Man's Land. Scottish soldier Alfred Anderson remembers shouting, "Merry Christmas!" to the soldiers in the German trenches. The British and German soldiers climbed out of their respective trenches, shook hands, sang a few carols, and even kicked a ball back and forth. By the afternoon, the merriness was over and machine-gun fire filled the air again, but the brief peace gave the soldiers a comforting reminder of better times. ✳

Christmas Stocking Story

For many folks around the world, hanging an oversize, colorful sock on the fireplace (or stairwell or doorknob) is a beloved Christmas tradition. After all, by Christmas morning, the stockings are filled with little treats and gifts—who wouldn't want to get in on that?

There are many theories behind why people hang Christmas stockings, but the one that seems to carry the most weight comes to us via an old folktale. In the story, a kindhearted but poor father had three daughters for whom he wished to find desirable husbands. The father was troubled, however, since he had no money for a dowry for even one of his

sweet, loving daughters. Then one day, St. Nicolas of Myra (aka Saint Nicholas, aka Santa Claus) was passing through town and heard about the plight of the kind father. Since he knew the man would be too proud to accept charity, St. Nicholas slipped down the chimney in the middle of the night (saints can do stuff like that) and dropped gold coins into the daughters' stockings, which they had hung on the fireplace to dry. They found the coins in the morning and voilà! A dowry for each, which led to a happy marriage for each, too. The story spread far and wide, and folks everywhere started hanging stockings on the mantel, hoping for a little love from St. Nicholas themselves.

Clement Clarke Moore's famous poem "A Visit from St. Nicholas" (or "'Twas The Night Before Christmas") was written in 1829, and as anyone who knows the poem will remember, Moore wrote: "The stockings

Christmas stockings, c. 1896

were hung by the chimney with care in hopes that St. Nicholas soon would be there." The tradition was at least firmly entrenched by then, which suggests that it came to America long before. Stocking hanging might come from a Dutch tradition, which has children in Holland putting their wooden shoes out on Christmas Eve stuffed with straw for Saint Nicholas's donkeys. They'd put out a treat for St. Nick, too, and if he was pleased, St. Nick would leave them a little gift. Regardless of the origin, stockings are found all over the Western world. In Italy, La Befana (the "good witch") put sweets and small gifts in stockings. In Puerto Rico, kids put flowers and tasty greens under their beds for the camels of the Three Kings. French kids put their shoes out, and in America, monogrammed stockings are put out well in advance of Christmas Day, serving as part of the decoration that fills the house with holiday cheer and goodwill. ♣

Santa Claus... Indiana?

Since the 1920s, residents of Santa Claus, Indiana, have been reading letters to Santa and responding to them. The town of about 2,200—which is located near the Kentucky border—is home to the Santa Claus Museum. In years past, Santa Clausians responded to as many as three million letters per year, but now the volume is closer to fifteen thousand. The responses are framed by one of three form letters—even people in Santa Claus, Indiana, have real jobs and personal lives to attend to—but the letters are personalized, and the postmark is obviously quite distinctive. ✳

Santa Claus asking you to mail your packages early, 1921

The Scoop on Christmas... Poop?

The people of Catalonia, one of Spain's 17 autonomous communities, celebrate Christmas pretty much like the rest of the world. But they have one special holiday custom found almost nowhere else: the *Caga Tio*, or pooping log.

The specially designed logs, which often come with tiny legs, cute painted faces, and a beret, are offered for sale at the beginning of each holiday season. Beginning on December 8, at the start of the Feast of the Immaculate Conception, the children give the log a little "snack" each day and cover it with a blanket to keep it warm. As Christmas approaches, parents secretly substitute larger and larger logs to give

the impression that the Caga Tío is growing. Then, on Christmas Eve or Christmas Day, as the family sings, the covered log is placed midway in an unlit fireplace (if the household has one) and ordered to "defecate" while being struck with sticks. Hidden under the blanket is a selection of small treats, such as candy, nuts, coins, and dried fruit, which are shared by all family members. The fun is over when the Caga Tío "poops" a salted herring, which signifies that it is empty. (Don't tell, but the parents place it there!)

A similarly themed Catalonian Christmas custom is the *caganer*, or "pooper." Traditionally, this is a small wood or porcelain figurine of a person squatting, which is discreetly hidden in a dark corner of a nativity scene so as not to be disrespectful. In some parts of Catalonia, children make a holiday game of searching for the caganer in their family's nativity arrangement. The origins of the caganer tradition

are vague, but some believe it started among peasant farmers who believed the figure's fecal offerings would help ensure that their fields remained fertile and productive in the coming year.

Caganers have been a fixture of southwestern European nativity scenes since at least the 17th century, but in 2005, the city council in Barcelona commissioned a nativity scene and tried to quietly leave out the caganer. They claimed it had nothing to do with political correctness and that they were merely trying to show support for a new anti-public defecation law, but Barcelonans weren't buying it. They demanded their caganer back, and in 2006, he returned. 🌲

I'm Dreaming of a White (House) Christmas... the FDR years

The White House Christmas tree, 1934 or 1935

Eleanor Roosevelt being presented with a Christmas tree by a troop of Girl Scouts, 1933

The Roosevelt's 1937 Christmas card

Workers putting up wreaths at the White House , December 1937

The Community Christmas tree being decorated a day before it is lit up, December 1937

In 1938, the children of diplomats stationed in Washington D.C. gathered to say "Merry Christmas" in a radio broadcast.

Christmas Laughs

During the Christmas season, three men got onto an elevator: an honest politician, a generous lawyer, and Santa Claus. Sitting on the floor of the elevator was a $20 bill.

Who picked it up?

Santa, of course. The other two are just figments of the imagination! ✳

Not Quite Wonderful?

The Christmas season would not be complete without a viewing (or two or three) of *It's a Wonderful Life*. But Frank Capra's Christmas classic, while wonderful, contains some noticeable bloopers. This year, while you're watching the redemptive story unfold, why not add some fun and see if you can also identify some of these goofs? Here are just a few:

✳ Encore Performance: During the dance, when people start jumping into the pool, the same person jumps in twice. Whoops!

✳ Have I Seen You Before?: In another repeat performance, a dark-haired female extra (holding the brim of her hat) crosses through a scene, where

George is approaching Ernie's taxi, five times in 30 seconds!

✳ **Quitting Smoking?:** When George Bailey is a young man and Ol' Man Gower sends him to deliver a prescription, Gower's cigar disappears. Also, when George is talking to Violet in his office, his pipe disappears.

✳ **What's Your Name Again?:** In one scene, George addresses Violet (played by the actress Gloria Grahame) by the wrong name. He calls her Gloria.

✳ **Too Soon!:** The Coca-Cola thermometer on the wall of the drugstore (where young George is working in 1919) wasn't created until 1939!

✳ **Switcheroo:** The camera shows Clarence and George being thrown out of the bar, but in the next shot (when they land), they've switched places.

✳ **Accidental Snow:** George's car does not have much snow on it when he crashes it into a tree, but when he gets out to inspect his car, it is suddenly snow-covered.

Did You Know?

It's a Wonderful Life is considered a classic now, but it actually didn't do well at the box office when first released. In fact, it marked the start of a long slide in popularity for the famous director. Moviegoers rejected the film at the box office, and it lost money despite being nominated for five Oscars. Some hold that the audiences who embraced the filmmaker's uplifting messages in the previous decade had become jaded and weary after the horrors of World War II and found no use for what they now saw as Capra's naive encouragement. Others contend that George Bailey's discovery of what might have been is depicted as a nightmare of loss and bitterness that survivors of war and hard times didn't want to be reminded of.

Whatever the reason for its failure, it wasn't until the 1970s, when *It's a Wonderful Life* became a staple of holiday television programming, that Americans finally embraced Capra's heartwarming Christmas flick.

• •

Speaking of Christmas flicks, *Miracle on 34th Street,* starring Maureen O'Hara and a young Natalie Wood, also premiered in 1947. June 1947, to be exact. We're…not sure why it premiered in June rather than, say, December. 🎄

Hopping Up the Wrong Tree

When relocating to a new home, most people rent a moving van, but when Pacific Chorus frogs want to move, apparently they just hitch a ride on Christmas trees bound for Alaska. In December 2009, the *Anchorage Daily News* reported that some of these critters were showing up in the Anchorage area during the holiday season, having traveled discreetly on trees imported from Oregon. (Who knows, maybe they just wanted to see the Northern Lights or go whale watching!)

Unfortunately for the Pacific Chorus frogs, city officials didn't exactly leap for joy at their arrival. In Alaska, these amphibians are nonnative and have

the potential to carry the disease-causing chytrid fungus, which has caused amphibian population declines around the world. Although the frogs didn't appear to be invasive, the Alaska Department of Fish and Game encouraged residents to take precautionary measures by killing the frogs (euthanizing them with a toothache anesthetic, such as Orajel) or putting them in the freezer. Then locals were supposed to bring in the frozen frogs for inspection. Not a very "hoppy" Christmas for these critters!

This wasn't the first time that Pacific Chorus frogs traveled far from home. In 2007, members of this North American species showed up in Guam—again riding Christmas trees. Maybe this time they were in search of sandy beaches and mangrove forests! ✳

Crunching the Christmas Numbers

1,175: Number of carolers present for the world's largest caroling service on December 20, 2003; the event was organized by the city of Cambridge in Ontario, Canada, and the carolers sang in the square for 28 minutes

100,000: Number of people who work in the Christmas tree industry in the United States

450: Number of figures in the world's largest diorama of the Nativity in Einsiedeln, Switzerland

Young Christmas carolers, c. 1890

Christmas Tree Facts

✳ The first Christmas tree was decorated in Riga, Latvia, in 1510.

✳ The first printed reference to Christmas trees occurred in Germany in 1531.

✳ In the United States, commercial Christmas trees have been around since 1850. The first commercial Christmas tree lot was established in New York in 1851 by entrepreneur Mark Carr.

✳ An estimated 25 to 30 million real trees are sold in the United States each year.

✳ There are an estimated 15,000 Christmas tree growers in the United States. The industry employs approximately 100,000 people.

✳ Christmas trees are commercially grown in every state, including Hawaii.

Christmas trees on their way for delivery, c. 1910

✳ Oregon is the leading grower of Christmas trees, producing more than six million trees each year. Other top tree-producing states include North Carolina, Pennsylvania, Michigan, and Virginia.

✳ Several different types of trees are sold commercially as Christmas trees. The most popular are Scotch pine, Douglas fir, Noble fir, and Fraser fir.

✳ On a typical Christmas tree farm, approximately 2,000 trees are planted per acre. Of that number, only 1,000 to 1,500 will survive.

✳ Every day, an acre of Christmas trees provides enough oxygen to support 18 people.

✳ It can take up to ten years for a Christmas tree to grow large enough for harvesting. However, the average is seven years. For every tree harvested, two to three saplings are planted the following season.

At the Christmas tree lot, c. 1920

Under the Christmas Tree: 1983

Cabbage Patch Kids are cloth dolls invented by Debbie Morehead and Xavier Roberts and first sold at craft shows in Kissimmee, Florida. Roberts eventually sold them at an old medical clinic he renamed the Babyland General Hospital, and adoption papers were provided for each doll. Coleco bought the line in 1982, gave the dolls plastic faces, and changed the name to Cabbage Patch Kids. They were introduced at the International Toy Fair in New York City in 1983, and by October they were sold out in most stores, causing massive crowds whenever a few were spotted for sale.

Cabbage Patch kids weren't the only game in town in the 1980s. The Care Bears started out as cuddly cartoon characters on greeting cards from American Greetings. In 1983, stuffed Care Bears toys were marketed by Parker Brothers and Kenner in conjunction with their first TV special, *The Land Without Feelings*. Care Bears were a popular toy that Christmas and over 40 million were sold between 1983 and 1987. More TV shows, movies, and the greeting cards have helped the Care Bears remain on the market. ♠

I'm Dreaming of a White (House) Christmas... 1975

First Lady Betty Ford joining Santa and a group of Diplomatic Corps children, 1975

The spirit of Christmas is ageless, irresistible and knows no barriers. It reaches out to add a glow to the humblest of homes and the stateliest of mansions. It catches up saint and sinner alike in its warm embrace. It is the season to be jolly— but to be silent and prayerful as well.

I know this will be a particularly happy Christmas for me. I celebrate it surrounded by those I love and who love me. I celebrate it by joining with all of our citizens in observing a Christmas when Americans can honor the Prince of Peace in a nation at peace.

—from Gerald Ford's 1975 Christmas message ❄

Christmas Crimes?!

Sometimes one more Christmas decoration is just one too many. In January 2008, a home security camera in Calgary, Alberta, captured footage of a man slashing through a couple's outdoor Christmas decorations with a machete. The huge inflatable Santa, polar bear, and train belonged to a mild-mannered couple. The camera didn't get a very good look at the grinch who also destroyed the sound system playing holiday classics, and the masked bandit responsible has yet to be brought to justice. 🎄

✴ In Maine, you are open to getting a fine if you leave your Christmas decorations up after January 14.

✴ In 1659, early American Puritans actually succeeded in banning Christmas altogether in Massachusetts.

✴ In Louisiana, a woman set up Christmas lights that were in the shape of a middle finger—pointing at her neighbors. The neighbors complained to the cops, who ordered the lights taken down, but a judge later ruled that (in the absence of an obscenity statue in the jurisdiction) the woman had the legal right to keep the lights up!

Yes, Virginia

As the 19th century drew to a close, New York's *Sun* penny newspaper answered a query from a little girl, and in so doing, created a holiday tradition that continues to the present day.

Virginia O'Hanlon, an Upper West Side resident who had just celebrated her eighth birthday in 1897, was so delighted by her presents that she began to wonder what she might receive at Christmas. "[As] a child, I just existed from July to December, wondering what Santa Claus would bring me," O'Hanlon later revealed. "I think I was a brat." She worried whether Santa Claus even existed at all, because school friends had been saying otherwise. Virginia's father ducked the issue by telling her to ask the newspaper because "if you see it in the *Sun*, it's so."

Ah, those were less cynical times!

An unsigned September 21, 1897, *Sun* editorial (written by Francis Pharcellus Church) was entitled "Is There a Santa Claus?" (See page 188 for the full text.) It touched a nerve with the public. "Virginia," the piece begins, "your little friends are wrong." And later: "Yes, Virginia, there is a Santa Claus. He exists as certainly as love and generosity and devotion exist."

Readers asked for seasonal reprints of the editorial. By 1902, the *Sun* grudgingly noted, "This year requests for its reproduction have been so numerous that we yield." In 1924, the paper ran it as the lead editorial in the Christmas Eve edition, and the paper began routinely republishing the piece every Christmas season. Even after the *Sun* folded in 1950, other newspapers kept the custom going.

Virginia O'Hanlon, who grew up to become an educator, received correspondence about the letter throughout her life. In 1998, PBS's *Antiques Road-show* authenticated and appraised Virginia's original letter at $20,000-$30,000. Over a century later, the newspaperman's impassioned reply to a small child's question remains one of the most cherished Christmas messages ever published. ✳

(Left): Does Santa keep up with the latest technology? Well, he was already using the phone by 1897 when this picture was taken, so we vote yes!

Becoming Santa

A family with four children had a long and established tradition—each person would buy a gift for one other family member through a gift swap; Mom and Dad would also buy one big gift for each child. They'd all put the presents beneath the tree on Christmas Eve before going to bed.

During the night, "Santa" and "Mrs. Santa" would sneak in and leave an additional "goody bag" of candy, small toys, and fun trinkets for each child. Long after the youngest child had figured out that Santa and Mrs. Santa were really Mom and Dad, the tradition continued, even as each child went through a sullen teenager phase where they rolled their eyes (but were secretly pleased) with the toy cars, bouncy

balls, and other gadgets that Santa delivered each year without fail.

When the kids were in their late teens and early 20s, the parents had a difficult year. The father took a pay cut at his job; the mother had some health issues that racked up medical bills. At Thanksgiving, the parents told their kids that they would be cutting back on expenses that year—and that the "Santas" would be delivering a box of candy for the house to share on Christmas morning, but not much else. The kids were old enough to understand, they were sure.

On Christmas Eve, the parents went to bed, the wife tearing up a bit because for the first time, they weren't sneaking out after the kids fell asleep to play Santa. But lo and behold, when everyone gathered on Christmas morning, they found not five goody bags left by the tree, but many more than that!

Each of the children had decided independently that they would play Santa that year, and had not only filled bags for their brothers and sisters, but for their parents as well. They had all become Santa. 🎄

Carolers in Madison Square Garden, New Year, between 1910 and 1920

Singing of a Silent Night

"Silent Night" was first performed on Christmas Eve in 1818 at the small village St. Nicholas church in Oberndorf, Austria. It was composed for the guitar and sung by the assistant priest and the composer, choir director, Franz Gruber. ✳

Reindeer Games

All the facts about reindeer…

✳ Santa's actual reindeer were probably not reindeer at all, but a compilation of traits from several members of the deer family. In some pictures, the reindeer have white tails, which are not a trait of the Lapland reindeer, as well as the facial structure of an antelope.

✳ So much for those wild reindeer games—at least in Lapland. It seems that the last of the wild herds were hunted out around 1900. Around the same time, the U.S. government imported 1,300 reindeer from Siberia to Alaska to provide food for Eskimo peoples. Herds grew to a million over the next 30

We suppose Santa could have chosen turkeys to draw his sleigh instead…

years but were also decimated by white hunters. In 1972, Alaska wildlife officials set quotas to protect the remaining herds of reindeer.

We bet these 1941 Christmas travelers wished they could travel by reindeer instead…

✳ Well-endowed male reindeer use their imposing antlers like a shovel to break through the upper crust of snow to reach the vegetation underneath.

✳ Contrary to belief, reindeer don't run very fast. In fact, a normal-size deer could outrun a reindeer. And not only can reindeer swim, but their soft, hollow hair is buoyant.

✳ Talk about getting special perks from the guy in the red suit…Before a poem entitled "The Children's Friend" and then Clement Clarke Moore's "'Twas the Night Before Christmas," Santa had to hoof it from house to house. (Moore apparently drew inspiration from the previous poem.) Moore was the first to out-fit Santa with a sleigh and eight, albeit "tiny," reindeer.

I'll Be Home for Christmas

Written by Kim Gannon and Walter Kent, "I'll Be Home for Christmas" was recorded in 1943 by Bing Crosby. The song was hugely popular with American GIs during World War II, but it was actually banned from BBC broadcast in the UK—BBC was afraid the sometimes melancholy lyrics might damper morale! 🎄

Soldiers waiting for a Greyhound bus , December 1941

Taken in January 1943, the photograph shows a family receiving a gift from one of their sons in the service, stationed in Africa.

A sailor gets his gifts wrapped at the United Nations service center in December 1943.

Christmas in Space

In December 1965, astronauts Frank Borman and James Lovell, then aboard the *Gemini 7* spacecraft, asked NASA to play the Bing Crosby recording of "I'll Be Home for Christmas" for them. They returned home on December 18, 1965, having spent almost 14 days in space, the longest spaceflight up until that point.

December 1968 saw Borman and Lovell in space again, aboard *Apollo 8* along with Wllliam Anders. *Apollo 8's* mission—to orbit the moon and return safely—was vital to the American space program, but it barely registered on the public consciousness at the time. That changed on December 24 when Commander Frank Borman, Command Module Pilot Jim Lovell, and Lunar Module Pilot William Anders

greeted the world with a holiday message from lunar orbit.

During the presentation, the astronauts showed pictures of the earth and the moon as seen from their space capsule. "The vast loneliness is awe-inspiring," said Lovell, "and it makes you realize just what you have back there on earth." Anders took the mic: "For all the people on earth, the crew of *Apollo 8* has a message we would like to send you." The astronauts then took turns reading the first ten verses of the book of Genesis.

Though *Apollo 8* didn't garner nearly as much attention as Apollo, the Christmas message from its crew was viewed by an estimated one billion people around the world, making it the most widely watched television broadcast at the time. ✳

Under the Christmas Tree: 1996

A furry red Muppet monster on the children's show *Sesame Street*, Elmo became the hot Christmas gift in 1996 when Tyco released Tickle Me Elmo, a plush toy that giggled when squeezed once and shook and laughed hysterically when squeezed three times. The toys were in short supply because of unexpected demand, causing stores to raise prices and parents to fight over them. Injuries were common, and newspapers ran ads offering one doll for as much as $1,500. Elmo spawned other Muppet Tickle Me characters, and in 2006, Elmo became popular again as TMX (Tickle Me Extreme), with more actions such as rolling on the floor and pounding his furry fist. 🎄

Christmas Laughs

Little Sarah frowned deeply when she saw the Christmas table laden with food: turkey, mostaccioli, sweet potatoes, stuffing, green bean casserole.

"What's wrong, honey?" asked her mom. "Aren't you feeling well?"

"I just don't think Jesus would approve of green beans that's all," Sarah said. "If we have to have a vegetable, shouldn't it be Jesus' favorite?"

"I don't think the Bible says anything about a favorite vegetable," her mom said.

Sarah sighed deeply and informed her mother that, "Of course it does, Mom. It says right in the Bible, he came to bring peas on Earth!" ✳

A Little Math

In order to complete his visits on Christmas Eve, Santa Claus would have to stop at 822 houses per second, traveling at a speed of 650 miles per second. Let's hope he doesn't get pulled over. 🎄

Santa talking to children at Macy's department store, 1942.
The information notes that Macy had "two Santas,
concealed from one another by a labyrinth to prevent
disillusionment of the children."

Christmas Card Trivia

✸ The most expensive Christmas card is an antique card from 1843, auctioned in 2001 in England for $40,000 USD.

✸ It is estimated that 500 million e-cards are sent annually.

✸ The busiest day of the year for the U.S. Postal Service is December 17, when 275 million cards and letters—more than three times the average daily volume of 82 million—will be mailed. From Thanksgiving to Christmas, a whopping 20 billion pieces of mail, including packages, will be delivered by the U.S. Postal Service.

✸ In 1941, when the government issued an order to reduce paper by 25 percent, the greeting card industry successfully lobbied for greeting cards to be exempt. They launched the "Defense Stamp Christmas Cards" campaign, which promoted defense stamps and war bonds. Another campaign, "Greeting Cards in Wartime," was created on the premise that Christmas cards boosted soldier morale and helped families keep in touch with each other during the war.

Postal workers during the Christmas season, between 1910 and 1915

Got Your Goat?

Every year at Christmas, the Southern Merchants of Gävle, Sweden, erect a straw goat. Nearly every year, vandalism gets their goat.

The tradition of building a Swedish Yule goat began in 1966, and the tradition of vandalizing it started shortly thereafter. Some years the goat goes up in flames mere hours after it's erected. Other goats have been smashed, run over by cars, and had their legs removed. Sometimes, as in 2014, the goat survives—three attempts at arson, in 2014. Sometimes, as in 2015, the goat burns before it can be dismantled. Still, the town continues the tradition. If the goat is destroyed before St. Lucia Day (December 13), it is often rebuilt.

Advertising man Stig Gavlén came up with the idea of building the goat to attract people to Gävle businesses. The Southern Merchants, a local association, provided financing for the first goat— which was built by the local fire department—on December 1, 1966, and it went up in flames at midnight on New Year's Eve. Successive goats were also vandalized, to the point that the Southern Merchants stopped building them for 15 years, and the task fell to the Natural Science Club of the School of Vasa. Their goats, too, often succumbed to flames. In 2001, a tourist from Cleveland, Ohio, was apprehended and spent 18 days in jail for setting fire to the goat, but often the culprits are never caught. The city has experimented with fireproofing chemicals, but they discolor the straw. There have been Webcams on the goat, but vandals have tampered with those as well. It's safe to say that at this point, the Gävle goat is an endangered species! 🎄

Dickens Meets Star Trek

Star Trek fans are a devoted group, embracing all aspects of their favorite television show while eagerly creating new, original works of their own. Trekkers are especially fond of all things Klingon, so it should come as no surprise that someone finally wrote a stage production of Charles Dickens's *A Christmas Carol* performed almost entirely in the fictional alien tongue.

The Commedia Beauregard Theater, in conjunction with the IKV RakeHell of the Klingon Assault Group, has produced *A Klingon Christmas Carol* at venues in Minnesota's Twin Cities since 2007. The premise of the show is that the audience is attending a

production at the Vulcan Institute of Cultural Anthropology, where Klingon stories and their human counterparts are being studied. The Imperial Klingon Players perform a decidedly Klingon version of *A Christmas Carol* while a Vulcan anthropologist narrates. As most members of the audience do not speak fluent Klingon, English subtitles are projected on an overhead screen. In this version of the Dickens classic, a Klingon with neither honor nor courage is visited by the ghost of a dead comrade. Later, he is visited by the spirits of three Klingon warriors, who help him find the bravery he lacks.

Interestingly, this isn't the first Star Trek connection to *A Christmas Carol*. In 1999, actor Patrick Stewart portrayed Ebenezer Scrooge in a television production of the Christmas holiday favorite. That time, though, the dialogue was in easy-to-understand English. A Merry Christmas to all! ✳

Christmas Quotes

At Christmas I no more desire a rose than wish a snow in May's newfangled mirth; But like of each thing that in season grows.

—William Shakespeare ✸

At Christmas play and make good cheer, for Christmas comes but once a year.

—Thomas Tusser ✸

Heap on more wood! —the wind is chill;
But let it whistle as it will,
We'll keep our Christmas merry still.

—Sir Walter Scott ❄

c. 1923

Success. Four flights Thursday morning.
All against twenty-one-mile wind. Started from
level with engine power alone. Average speed
through air thirty-one miles. Longest fifty-nine
seconds. Inform press. Home Christmas.

—Telegram from Orville and Wilbur Wright to the
Reverend Milton Wright, from Kitty Hawk,
December 17, 1903 ❄

This 1900 image shows the Christmas tree in the Wright home in Dayton, Ohio.

Under the Christmas Tree: 1998

Talking Furby robots that had their own language and appeared to communicate with each other were the hit of the 1998 Christmas season. Invented by Dave Hampton and Caleb Chung, they debuted at the International Toy Fair in 1998 and quickly became the season's must-have toy, with 1.8 million Furbies sold in 1998 and a total of over 40 million in three years. Priced at $35, shortages caused some to be resold for over $300. 🎄

Under the Christmas tree, 1897

Christmas Around the World: *Italy*

For Italians, Christmas is a lengthy affair. The season begins on the first Sunday of Advent. Italians start everything off with a bang—literally. Fireworks are set off and bonfires are lit, and families shop for trees, gifts, food, and decorations for the house at the popular Christmas markets set up just for the holiday. As the weeks progress, kids take to the streets to sing carols, a tradition that began in Italy. Manger scenes are set up in yards, and children write down their Christmas wish lists on slips of paper in hopes that La Befana (the Italian version of Santa) will take note. She delivers gifts on Epiphany, the first week of January. Kids in Italy don't have to wait that long for gifts, though; Babbo Natale, aka

Father Christmas, brings small gifts to children on Christmas Day too. But the wish lists youngsters write down on slips of paper are for La Befana.

When Christmas Eve hits, it's all about the Nativity. Candles are lit, and the baby Jesus is passed from person to person in the family. After a meatless dinner, everyone heads to mass. On Christmas, traditional *panettone* (a sweetened bread with dried fruits—much lighter than fruitcake) is enjoyed, one small part of a feast large even by Italian standards. By the time New Year's Eve rolls around, everyone's pretty exhausted, but the Italians take New Year's Day as an opportunity to exchange gifts and reflect on the enjoyment of the holiday. But don't worry, the season isn't over yet. La Befana still has to swoop down on her broom to deliver gifts on January 6. ✳

Virgin Islands

North Americans think of pines when they think of Christmas trees, but the traditional Christmas tree in the Virgin Islands was the local inkberry tree. The inkberry tree grew in the wild and didn't need a lot of water.

Caroling is a long-standing tradition, as can be seen in this picture *(right)* that dates back to 1941. Lucky carolers would be welcomed into homes and fortified by treats of ham and sweet bread as they caroled. 🎄

Sweden

T hough Swedish celebrations begin on December 13, St. Lucia Day, the biggest celebration of the year is Christmas Eve—*Julafton*—when families feast on a traditional Swedish smorgasbord. Christmas ham, pickled pigs' feet, lutefisk (fish soaked in lye), boiled wheat (*cuccidata*), cabbage pudding, baby potatoes, sweet carrots, deviled eggs, saffron buns with raisins, lingonberry pie, pepparkakor (sweet ginger cookies), and rice pudding are part of a typical holiday meal. Of course, no party would be complete without glögg, a strong but sweet hot mulled wine that instantly warms the body.

Just after dinner, children look for *tomte* to arrive. These mischievous elves live underneath the floorboards but come out once a year to deliver presents on Christmas Eve to everyone. In the past, they were

thought to protect the livestock and children of farmers. One in particular, *Jultomte,* dresses much like Santa Claus in a red and white suit.

In the late evening and early morning, families head to church. The Twelve Days of Christmas and Epiphany follow in January, but the season doesn't end until St. Knut's Day on January 13. On this day, the 20th day after Christmas, with *knut* being the word for 20, families take down the Christmas tree and polish off any edible ornaments left over from the holiday. ✳

Boy of Portuguese descent with crèche, 1940

Portugal

One popular tradition in Portugal is the presépio, or nativity scene. Derived from the word "pre-sepium" (meaning a bed of straw where the Christ child lay), elaborate presépio pop up in many places throughout the Christmas season. Traditionally, children gather the materials for the crèche.

A traditional desert of the season is the "Bolo Rei," a sort of cake. The lucky eater finds a treat hidden in the cake. The unlucky one find a broad bean—meaning they have to buy the cake next year. 🌲

Japan

C hristmas is not a holiday generally associated with Japan. After all, less than one half of one percent of the nation's population are Christian. But as it turns out, this doesn't matter. While the Japanese may not be into the religious aspects of the holiday, they can't get enough of the celebration!

Indeed, Christmas is amazingly popular in the Land of the Rising Sun. While December 25 is not a national holiday there as it is in the United States, the people still like to go all-out in the spirit of the season. On Christmas Eve, for example, it's traditional for the entire family to enjoy a special Christmas cake, which the father purchases on his way home from work.

Christmas Eve is also promoted as a day for romance. Young lovers use the holiday as an excuse for a romantic interlude, filling fancy restaurants and expensive hotels, while those at the beginning of a relationship may use it as an opportunity to express their true feelings. As a result, asking someone out on Christmas Eve has implications far deeper than just dinner and a movie.

Speaking of dinner, chicken has become the meal of choice on Christmas Day for many Japanese—thanks to some savvy marketing by Kentucky Fried Chicken! So popular has the Christmas chicken dinner become in Japan that families often place their orders well in advance so they don't miss out. ✳

Greece

The Greeks love their customs and traditions—especially when it comes to Christmas! Here are just a few:

St. Nicholas is the holiday's patron saint—but he's also the protector of sailors, so you're just as likely to see a boat decorated with colorful lights as a traditional Christmas tree.

Unlike the United States, where gifts are traditionally given on Christmas Eve or Christmas Day, in Greece they are given on New Year's Day. As a result, Christmas shopping continues long after Christmas itself. While Christmas carols may be sung anytime during the holiday, there are actually three official caroling days: Christmas Eve, New Year's Eve, and January 5, which is the Eve of the Epiphany. On these special

occasions, children carrying triangles go from house to house singing carols, and they are given money or treats as rewards.

Some people hang a pomegranate above the front door of their house so that it has dried by New Year's Day. To ensure good luck during the coming year, the dried pomegranate is thrown on the ground so that it breaks, then everyone steps into their homes with their right foot first.

On January 6, at the end of the Christmas season, local waters are blessed and a wood cross is thrown in. Then dozens of young men jump into the frigid waters in an attempt to retrieve it. Why? Because whoever reaches the cross first will have a year of good luck. 🎄

Brazil

Brazilians don't associate Christmas with snow and "Jack Frost nipping at your nose." That's because it's summer in the South American country, and even Papai Noel (the Brazilian version of Santa Claus, imported from North America in the 1950s) has to dress in a lightweight silk suit to keep cool. Some people celebrate the holiday by hitting the beach and watching fireworks or having a BBQ.

Some Brazilians enact the traditional play *Los Pastores* ("The Shepherds"), which is also performed in Mexico—except Brazil's version features shepherd-esses instead of shepherds and a gypsy who sneaks in and tries to snatch baby Jesus from his straw bed!

Many Brazilians celebrate the holiday by exchanging clues with an *amigo secreto* (a "Secret Santa" of

sorts) whose identity is not revealed until Christmas, accompanied by the giving of a special gift. Up until that point, participants conceal their identity by corresponding with fake names.

The Christmas meal is often a lavish affair, featuring roast turkey and ham, seasonal fruits and vegetables, beans, and rice. Some families attend mass on December 24 and then eat their special dinner at midnight. Others attend midnight mass or *Missa do Galo* (*galo* meaning "rooster," since the service traditionally ends at 1 A.M.), although this mass is no longer as widely observed. As is the tradition in many countries, on Christmas morning, children open presents that were delivered in the night by Papai Noel. ✳

Ethiopia

C hristmas in the African country of Ethiopia is
called Ganna and takes place on January 7,
since Ethiopians observe the ancient Julian calendar.
It is largely a religious celebration. The day before
Ganna, people fast and then, early the next morning,
dress in white clothing. Some also don a traditional
shamma, a thin cotton cloth resembling a toga that
has colorful stripes along the hem.

For the faithful in Ethiopia, there's no sleeping in on
Christmas morning: Mass takes place at 4 A.M.! In rural areas, services are often held in ancient churches
carved out of volcanic rock, while in urban centers,
mass is held in modern churches designed in three
concentric circles. Upon entering the church, each
person is given a candle and then solemnly circles
the sanctuary three times before taking his or her

place in the second circle (the choir occupies the outer circle). Men and women are separated, and in the inner circle, the priest serves Holy Communion. The mass can last up to three hours, and everyone stands throughout. After church, young men play a game, also called *Ganna*, which is similar to hockey.

Twelve days after Christmas, on January 19, Ethiopians observe *Timkat,* a three-day celebration of the baptism of Christ. The priests wear white and red robes and carry intricately embroidered umbrellas. This time, the young men play a jousting game called *yeferas guks.* In Ethiopia, gift-giving is not a large part of the celebration, though children do receive simple presents. Instead, families partake in religious rituals, games, and shared meals. 🎄

Poland

As in many European countries, Christmas in Poland starts well before Christmas Day, during Advent. Church is held each day before dawn, and carolers stroll the streets singing of Christ's birth. Christmas trees are decorated with apples, walnuts, chocolate, and handmade ornaments called *pajaki*, made from eggshells and clay. The weeks leading up to Christmas are filled with special Polish foods including *oplatek*, a thin wafer pressed into a tin that forms the image of the Nativity or another holy image. The wafers are then shared among families and neighbors as a gesture of glad tidings.

Polish folks pull out all the stops for Christmas Eve supper. The meatless feast consists of 12 dishes representing the 12 months. Of course, no Polish meal would be complete without *pierogi,* or dumplings.

The Christmas season has long been one full of superstition and fortune-telling, though not as strongly observed today. During Advent and some-times on Christmas Eve, beeswax is dripped into a bowl of water, and fortunes are told from the shapes that emerge. Some rural residents still claim that on Christmas Eve animals are able to speak in a human tongue; some also claim that maidens can foretell their marriage date by eavesdropping on the neigh-bors and listening for specific words in their conver-sation.

While many Polish Christmas superstitions have faded away, plenty of modern-day Poles still believe that "as goes Christmas Eve, so goes the year." This means that to ensure a good coming year, everyone tries to be extra polite and generous on that day, forgiving each other in the name of the special season. ✳

Mexico

C hristmas festivities kick into high gear mid-month with *Las Posadas*. As colorful as carnival, this beloved nine-day event began eons ago as a way to help children learn the Nativity story. Starting at dusk on December 16, children dress in bright costumes and parade throughout their neighborhood from one house to another. Little girls vie for the role of the Virgin Mary, who gets to lead the parade through the streets riding a burro led by a boy playing Joseph. A host of heavenly angels carrying candles and Wise Men bearing gifts follow close behind. Moving down the street, the procession stops at houses along the route to request shelter at the inn—the *posada*—for the night. Like the Holy Family, they are turned away several times. At the last stop, which is often unannounced, the doors fling open to welcome the group inside. A party with refreshments or dinner usually follows, with children each getting a turn to break open a piñata.

In many homes, nativities, or *crèches,* are displayed prominently—at times taking up the entire room. While the Holy Family remains the focal point, entire flocks of sheep and livestock accompanied by shepherds, a host of angels, and other villagers join them in the midst of a true-to-life landscape. Small stables and workshops are tucked between waterfalls, cacti, and palm trees. Only on Christmas Eve, when the baby Jesus is tucked into the manger, is the scene finally complete. 🎄

Under the Christmas Tree: 1989

C hristmas 1989 was the first time many kids found a handheld video game player under the tree. The Nintendo Game Boy was released in North America on July 31, 1989, and it became an immediate hit. The Game Boy was priced at $109, powered by four AA batteries, and included Tetris, a puzzle game. Other games could be loaded using miniature cartridges. The monochrome Game Boy was replaced by the Game Boy Color in 1998. ✳

Under the Christmas tree, c. 1908

Santa's Evil Twin

In Germany, Austria, and other parts of Europe, there's a dark side to the holiday, and his name is Krampus.

The legend of Krampus (which is derived from the German word *"krampen,"* which means claw) originated in the alpine regions of Germany, and it spread throughout Austria, Hungary, Bavaria, and Slovenia. Simply speaking, Krampus, who is believed to be based in part on the Norse god Loki, is an evil spirit with thick fur and large, menacing horns who delights in punishing bad children as much as Santa Claus enjoys giving gifts to those who are good. In some regions, Krampus is considered Santa's evil twin, accompanying St. Nick on his rounds.

In his earliest incarnations, Krampus was frequently viewed from a much more adult perspective. A product of ancient European pagan practices, he was very sexual by nature, and early depictions of the naughty spirit often showed him advancing on women. His leering expression and wagging tongue clearly gave away his lascivious intent. Krampus remains especially popular in Austria, where Krampus Night celebrations are held every December 5, the eve of St. Nicholas Day. Traditionally, young men dress up as the evil spirit and roam the streets frightening children and young women, sometimes gently (or not so gently) smacking them with a whip.

In Hungary, Krampus isn't quite as nasty. Over the years, his image has softened a bit, and he is more commonly considered a sly trickster rather than an outright evil spirit. But his mission is the same: to encourage children to be good. 🎄

Between 1921 and 1924

Christmas Tree Lights

A Christmas tree wouldn't be the same without lights, now would it? Before electricity, folks lit their trees by placing small candles on the branches, which as you can imagine is pretty dangerous. Lanterns were used around the turn of the 20th century, but a few years before that, in 1882, the first Christmas tree was lit by electricity. The man who did it was named Edward Johnson, and he created the first string of electric lights by hand-wiring red, white, and blue bulbs. Within a matter of years, his invention was being mass-produced and people everywhere were lighting their trees with tiny glowing bulbs. The lights weren't fail-safe, however; in 1917, an inventor named Albert Sadacca developed a safer string of lights and became a millionaire when he developed something else the world loved to see—colored bulbs. ✳

Christmas Laughs

Grandma went "hmph" when her grandchildren started talking about the three wise men. "Wise men?!" she said. "What kind of use were their gifts? What baby needs gold instead of a onesie?"

"Oh Mom," her daughter said.

"I'm just saying," Grandma said. "If there had been three wise women, they would have brought a casserole, some clothes, and a diaper! Not to mention, they would have asked directions and arrived on time to help deliver the baby!" 🎄

Maybe this 1897 Grandma is giving out presents. Maybe she's critiquing the gift choices of the wise men. Who knows?

Christmas Games of Yore

W hether it's a snowy round of capture the flag on the lawn, a board game marathon, or classic hide-and-seek with the kids, Christmas is a time for play. Here are some of history's traditional Christmas games.

Blindman's bluff: Whoever is "it" is blindfolded. That person then gropes around the room, trying to make contact with the other, nonblindfolded players—who try not to get caught. This game was popular during Henry VIII's reign and has been a holiday favorite for many years, especially for young people during the Victorian era.

Stoolball: In 1621, the governor of the British Colony of Massachusetts ordered the citizens of Plymouth to stop playing games on Christmas Day, deeming

it unholy. One of the rowdy games he put an end to was stoolball. The game went like this: A milking stool was used as a target, and a hard leather ball stuffed with either hair or feathers was thrown at it. One player pitched the ball; another defended the stool with a bat made of wood. Sound familiar? This game evolved over the years to something we call "baseball."

Pitching the bar: This was another Christmastime game Puritan leaders put a stop to, at least for awhile. "Pitching the bar" was essentially a game of strength, where the typically male players would heave a log over their shoulder, similar to events in logger games today.

Cat's cradle: This play-anywhere string game was originally known as "cratch cradle," referring to the Christ child's cratch, or manger. The shape of the strings, once intertwined between fingers, resemble the wooden crossbracing of the manger. The name of the game evolved to "cat's cradle," but its origin is definitely Christmas-based. ✳

The Greatest Gift
That Wasn't

On Christmas morning 1977, thousands of American children woke up to find an empty box under the tree, and to them, it was the greatest gift ever. But this box wasn't exactly empty: It contained a certificate for the first four toys in a line that would become one of the most popular ever. These children were the first generation of *Star Wars* fans.

Prior to obtaining the license to produce *Star Wars* action figures, Kenner was a small toy company from Ohio owned by General Mills. Its most popular products up until then were classics such as Play-Doh, the Easy-Bake Oven, and the Spirograph. In 1975, the company achieved some success with licensed properties when it made the *Six Million Dollar Man*

toys. They sold well enough to help Kenner break the $100 million mark for the first time. It wasn't too much of a surprise then that the company would take a chance on George Lucas's little science-fiction adventure a couple of years later.

Unfortunately, Kenner wasn't expecting the film to do well and hadn't begun production on any *Star Wars* toys when the film came out, and several months later it still wasn't ready to meet the demand for Christmas. *Star Wars* had already broken all box-office records, but without a toy to put under the tree, it looked like Kenner and *Star Wars* would miss the chance to capitalize on the biggest movie phenomenon since *Gone with the Wind*. With nothing to lose, Kenner decided to sell little more than the promise of a toy. The IOU came in the form of a certificate good for four action figures to be shipped between February and June of 1978. The company sold it as the "Early Bird Certificate Package,"

which included little more in the package than the certificate and a few stickers. Demand was high for *Star Wars* toys though, so Kenner did all it could to get the word out to the good little boys and girls of the world. In the next year, the company's profits would double thanks to *Star Wars*.

Kenner started an advertising campaign that included television commercials, print ads, and a catalog. TV spots showed two happy children, gleefully extending Luke Skywalker's lightsaber, twisting R2-D2's dome, and posing the wookie Chewbacca with Princess Leia. The Kenner catalog had more details though, and it listed the certificate and stickers, as well as a *Star Wars* Club membership card. The commercial alerted kids to a delivery date between February and June of the following year, and the catalog revealed another important fact: The soon-to-be famous "*Star Wars* Empty Box" would only be sold until December 31, 1977. It wasn't long before print ads began running as well. One Kenner ad even upped the ante, promising delivery of all toys by February 15, 1978, a much quicker timeframe than the prospect of getting the toys nearly a year after the film debuted.

Today, the *Star Wars* Early Bird Certificate Package can be difficult to come by in its original condition. Nearly all those purchased in 1977 were torn open, the stickers stuck to lunch boxes, and the certificates mailed away for the promised figures. Those four toys that came, however, still fetch a good price on Web sites such as eBay. It's easy to see why so many would pay so much for something so little. For many, remembering the excitement that came from opening an empty box on Christmas morning is priceless. ♣

Christmas tableaux, late 1930s

Lawn Ornaments

Way back in 1223, St. Francis of Assisi held the first ever nativity scene in a cave in Italy. He used real, live people to depict the scene of Christ's birth as a way to remind people of the meaning of Christmas. Live nativity scenes caught on, but eventually the scenes were arranged with statues. These could be said to have been the first Christmastime lawn ornaments. Once the Industrial Revolution happened and mass commercialization really fired up, producing lots and lots of holiday statues became easier—and the more variety the manufacturer could offer, the more money he'd make. Thus, your neighbors next door feel compelled to light the block with an inflatable Rudolph, that twirling Santa, a blinking Frosty, and…✳

Christmas Windows

I f you've ever been downtown in a large city around the holidays, you've likely gone to check out the window displays created by the big department stores. Those fantasyland scenes that inspire thousands of Christmas lists every year were born not so very long ago.

In Chicago in the mid-1800s, there was a shopping revolution afoot. Marshall Field's flagship location on Chicago's bustling State Street boasted, over the years, the first escalator, the first bridal registry, and the first personal shoppers (a free service. In 1897, the popular store pioneered window display design, too. Up until then, window displays were heavy on product and light on art; in 1897, Field hired a full-time window designer named Arthur Fraser to focus on making the windows of the State Street store works of art, not just product displays. He figured it would draw more business, and it did; it also became a destination spot for Chicagoans and visitors from around the world. 🎄

Macy's toy window, between 1908 and 1917

Putting together a Christmas list…

A display at an Oldsmobile dealer's, c. 1921.
We're not sure Santa will be able to get down the chimney
with a car blocking his way—unless he upgraded from
reindeer and that's his car!

Christmas Quotes

Happy, happy Christmas, that can win us back to the delusions of our childhood days, recall to the old man the pleasures of his youth, and transport the traveler back to his own fireside and quiet home!

—Charles Dickens ❄

Christmas is a season not only of rejoicing but of reflection.

—Winston Churchill ❄

The earth has grown old with its burden of care, but at Christmas it always is young, the heart of the jewel burns lustrous and fair, and its soul full of music breaks the air, when the song of angels is sung.

—Phillips Brooks ❄

Leaving Christmas Day service, 1941

Down the Chimney

For somebody who is supposed to be such a magical, all-knowing being, it appears that Santa Claus possibly isn't very bright. Case in point: this chimney business. Come on, Claus. Do you really need to shimmy down a filthy chimney to deliver your presents?

In Santa's defense, there's a lot of tradition behind his chimney act. Back in pre-Christian Europe, Germanic people celebrated the winter solstice at the end of December with a holiday known as Yule. Christmas, which later supplanted the pagan winter solstice festivals during the Christianization of Germanic people, maintained many of the pagan traditions. One was the belief that at Yule-time, the god Odin would ride a magical eight-legged horse through the sky. Children left food for the horse, which would

Caught
in the
Act

The writing on this 1900 image reads, "Caught in the Act"!

Do I hear something?

be replaced by gifts from Odin, a custom that lives on today in the form of cookie bribery for Kris Kringle and his flying reindeer.

As for sliding down the chimney, folklorists point to another Germanic god: Hertha, the goddess of the home. In ancient pagan days, families gathered around the hearth during the winter solstice. A fire was made of evergreens, and the smoke beckoned Hertha, who entered the home through the chimney to grant winter solstice wishes.

••

Santa's fate was sealed when literature professor Clement Clarke Moore penned the 1822 poem "Twas the Night Before Christmas." Santa sliding down the chimney became a permanent fixture in popular Christmas tradition. ✳

Under the Christmas Tree: 2005

Microsoft unveiled the Xbox 360 videogame console on May 12, 2005, to replace the original Xbox. It was not released to the American public until November 22, 2005, causing a huge rush of Christmas purchases that Microsoft underestimated. At one point, an estimated 10 percent of all Xbox 360s available were on sale through online auction sites. By the end of the year, over 900,000 had been sold in the United States. 🎄

Christmas Laughs

Two little brothers were spending Thanksgiving weekend at their grandparents' home. When bedtime came, they knelt to say their night prayers. The older boy began to say very loudly, "I PRAY FOR A NEW BIKE FOR CHRISTMAS."

The younger boy said, "Why are you talking so loud? God isn't deaf, and neither's Santa."

The older boy replied, "No, but Grandma is!" ✳

"Yes, Virginia" Editorial, New York's Sun newspaper, September 21, 1897

VIRGINIA, your little friends are wrong. They have been affected by the skepticism of a skeptical age. They do not believe except they see. They think that nothing can be which is not comprehensible by their little minds. All minds, Virginia, whether they be men's or children's, are little. In this great universe of ours man is a mere insect, an ant, in his intellect, as compared with the boundless world about him, as measured by the intelligence capable of grasping the whole of truth and knowledge.

Yes, VIRGINIA, there is a Santa Claus. He exists as certainly as love and generosity and devotion exist, and you know that they abound and give to your life its highest beauty and joy. Alas! how dreary would be the world if there were no Santa Claus. It would be as dreary as if there were no VIRGINIAS. There would be no childlike faith then, no poetry, no romance to make tolerable this existence. We should have no enjoyment, except in sense and sight. The eternal light with which childhood fills the world would be extinguished.

Not believe in Santa Claus! You might as well not believe in fairies! You might get your papa to hire men to watch in all the chimneys on Christmas Eve to catch Santa Claus, but even if they did not see Santa Claus coming down, what would that prove? Nobody sees Santa Claus, but that is no sign that there is no Santa Claus. The most real things in the world are those that neither children nor men can see.

Did you ever see fairies dancing on the lawn? Of course not, but that's no proof that they are not there. Nobody can conceive or imagine all the wonders there are unseen and unseeable in the world.

You may tear apart the baby's rattle and see what makes the noise inside, but there is a veil covering the unseen world which not the strongest man, nor even the united strength of all the strongest men that ever lived, could tear apart. Only faith, fancy, poetry, love, romance, can push aside that curtain and view and picture the supernal beauty and glory beyond. Is it all real? Ah, VIRGINIA, in all this world there is nothing else real and abiding.

No Santa Claus! Thank God! he lives, and he lives forever. A thousand years from now, Virginia, nay, ten times ten thousand years from now, he will continue to make glad the heart of childhood. ★

How Do You Say Merry Christmas?

Afrikaans: Geseënde Kersfees
Albanian: Gezur Krislinjden
Arabic: Milad Majid
Bengali: Shubho borodin
Bulgarian: Tchestita Koleda; Tchestito Rojdestvo Hristovo
Catalan: Bon Nadal
Croatian: Sretan Bozic
Czech: Prejeme Vam Vesele Vanoce
Danish: Glædelig Jul
Ethiopian (Amharic): Melkin Yelidet Beaal
Farsi: Cristmas-e-shoma mobarak bashad
Finnish: Hyvaa joulua
French: Joyeux Noël
Gaelic: Nollaig chridheil agus Bliadhna mhath ùr!

German: Fröhliche Weihnachten
Haiti (Creole): Jwaye Nowel
Hungarian: Kellemes Karacsonyi unnepeket
Icelandic: Gledileg Jol
Indonesian: Selamat Hari Natal
Italian: Buone Feste Natalizie or Buon Natale
Korean: Sung Tan Chuk Ha
Lao: souksan van Christmas
Latin: Natale Hilare
Latvian: Prieci'gus Ziemsve'tkus
Macedonian: Sreken Bozhik
Navajo: Merry Keshmish
Norwegian: God Jul or Gledelig Jul
Filipino: Maligayang Pasko
Portuguese: Feliz Natal
Romanian: Craciun fericit
Russian: Pozdrevlyayu s prazdnikom Rozhdestva
Spanish: Feliz Navidad
Swedish: God Jul
Vietnamese: Chuc Mung Giang Sinh
Welsh: Nadolig Llawen